NICK WHITBY

Nick Whitby has had his plays produced on the Edinburgh
Fringe, at the Old Red Lion, Boulevard, and Donmar
Warehouse in London, in Sydney, at the Writers' Theatre,
Chicago, on Broadway and in around forty major productions in
Europe, including the Schiller and Gorky Theatres in Berlin, the
Josefstadt Vienna and the national theatres of Prague and
Krakow. He has written for various comedians, and in most
formats for television, including sketches, sitcom, drama,
comedy-drama, animation and documentary, and the odd bit of
radio and film. He lives with his family in the far west of
Cornwall, about two hours from England by train.

Other Titles in this Series

Nick Whitby

THE COMPLAINT

NICK HERN BOOKS

London

www.nickhernbooks.co.uk

A Nick Hern Book

The Complaint first published in Great Britain in 2012 as a paperback original by Nick Hern Books Limited, 14 Larden Road, London W3 7ST, in association with Hampstead Theatre

Cover image: © iStockphoto.com
Cover design: Ned Hoste, 2H

Typeset by Nick Hern Books, London
Printed in the UK by Mimeo Ltd, Huntingdon, Cambridgeshire PE29 6XX

A CIP catalogue record for this book is available from the British Library

ISBN 978 1 84842 275 9

In fondest memory of the potter and teacher
Tom Fisher

Author's Note

The Complaint is a play about an individual taking on a
bureaucracy – in the tradition of Franz Kafka, and others –
written in 2011 during the Arab Spring and the Greek financial
crisis. Some years before, I'd been living in Cairo and had spent
many bewildering days in El Mogamma, Egypt's vast and
imposing interior ministry building on Tahrir Square at which
the 2011 protests were aimed. The strange connection between
these events and the West's rearguard defence of its worldly
position lies at the heart of the play. *The Complaint*, however, is
actually a reversal of Kafka's model, and also why it's in
dramatic form (rather than a novel). In that world the
protagonist is typically baffled and thwarted by an impenetrable
and sinister administration seen through the prism of the
protagonist's mind. The play, however, works in the opposite
way. The administration is in the state of angst, and it's the
individual who holds the mystery.

A note on production: casting should be racially and culturally
broad and carefully balanced to suggest a range of geographical
settings. This ambiguity should be supported by the music
bridging the scenes, ideally played live with several
instruments; but where this is impractical, played by a solo
musician on, for instance, a zokra (Arabic oboe/clarinet), pipes,
or accordion. This music should start somewhere in the
Southern Mediterranean, travel east, up into Turkey, the
Balkans and Southern Europe, west to Spain, and the Atlantic
Coast. The same eclectic principle could apply to the design,
which might appear at times quite alien and hard to pin down, at
others quite familiar. Together, these elements should support a
sense of a world that's both close and yet a little removed,
possibly in time. Now and again the play becomes openly
comic, but it's advised this should never be too strongly played.

Nick Whitby

The Complaint was first performed at Hampstead Theatre
Downstairs, London, on 17 May 2012, with the following cast:

AFRA   Zora Bishop
MR TABUTANZER   Peter Bankole
TRUMAN   Callum Dixon
DAWN BIRDCATCHER   Nathalie Armin

Director   Simon Usher
Designer   Anthony Lamble
Lighting Designer   Simon Bennison
Sound Designer   Paul Bull
Production Manager   John Pitt

Characters

AFRA, *in her twenties*
MR TABUTANZER, *in his thirties*
TRUMAN, *in his late thirties or older*
DAWN BIRDCATCHER, *in her late twenties or
early/mid-thirties*

*This text went to press before the end of rehearsals and so may
differ slightly from the play as performed.*

Scene One

*An office with a hot, tropical bareness about it; a plain desk,
two wooden chairs, and a slowly rotating ceiling fan. A formal
framed photo of a sashed head-of-state hangs on a wall. Blinds
separate the room from two other offices at the back/sides.
Largely hidden behind these blinds are two barely discernible
figures at work. In the main office,* MR TABUTANZER *is
revealed at the desk that's clear except for an intercom/phone,
and an open laptop. On one of the wooden chairs,* AFRA *is
sitting, facing him. It is extremely hot and humid and both of
them shine with perspiration, their clothes sweat-stained. Both
repeatedly wipe themselves with hankies/towels.* MR
TABUTANZER *is looking (not unpleasantly) between* AFRA
*and the file of notes on the desk. When he speaks it's with the
distinct patterns (and sometimes unusual emphases) of an
African.*

MR TABUTANZER. They say it will get warmer over the next
four months. That is until the end of August or the beginning
of September, and then it will become quite cool again. Your
complaint was made on the first of December?

AFRA. Yes.

MR TABUTANZER *counts on his fingers.*

MR TABUTANZER. Twenty-two weeks. Usually a complaint
will perish before it reaches twenty weeks. But I think we
can say that yours is established. Is this your first?

AFRA. Yes.

MR TABUTANZER. I thought so.

After a silence.

You wish to go through with this, truly?

AFRA. I do.

MR TABUTANZER *takes an alcoholic hand-cleanser from a desk drawer and cleans his hands methodically before returning it and lifting the desk phone, pressing a button.*

MR TABUTANZER. I need a DV30.

He replaces the receiver, and takes out a packet from another drawer. He opens this and removes a pair of white sterilised reading gloves, putting these on through the following.

You will have to answer a few questions.

TRUMAN *enters carrying a brown A4 envelope. He hands it to* MR TABUTANZER, *all the time glaring at* AFRA *with inexplicable malevolence.*

Thank you.

TRUMAN *goes, continuing to glare at* AFRA, *making her uncomfortable.* MR TABUTANZER *takes the envelope, blows dust off it, opens it, and tips out a form and a piece of string onto the desk.*

Please, draw your chair closer. These are simply formalities, so that your complaint may proceed in a merry fashion. If you cannot answer a question we shall return to it at the end, if there's time.

AFRA. Time?

MR TABUTANZER. There is a time limit. (*Noting it down off his digital watch, which he sets.*)

AFRA. Why?

MR TABUTANZER. So that it's fair on the others. Although in this case there are no others. Forgive me, it's been so long since anyone has brought a complaint. (*After staring at her, he reads.*) Date... we have established that... (*Writes.*) December... da-di-da... Your name... (*Fills in.*) and also I shall need the name and address of your closest living relative. Just there... after... no, no don't touch the paper!

He waits as she fills these in.

Very good. (*Takes back the form and the pen, disposes of the pen and takes another out of a wrapper.*) Are you married?

AFRA. No.

MR TABUTANZER. Cohabiting?

AFRA. No.

MR TABUTANZER. Are you seeing someone on a regular or a semi-regular basis?

AFRA (*hesitates*). Yes.

MR TABUTANZER. An irregular basis? I shall put 'yes' but with two e's and a dash between the e's, to give a sense of uncertainty. (*Does so.*) How would you describe your relations with this person?

AFRA. I wouldn't.

MR TABUTANZER. Not at all?

AFRA. Not unless I had to. Do I have to?

MR TABUTANZER *reads on. After a moment…*

MR TABUTANZER. No. Have you ever suffered from malaria?

AFRA. Never.

MR TABUTANZER. 'Poss-ib-ly…' (*Ticks again.*) Question three. Katharine Hepburn or Spencer Tracy?

AFRA. I'm sorry?

MR TABUTANZER. Which would you favour, for example, in a divorce settlement?

AFRA *looks blank.* MR TABUTANZER *leans forward confidentially.*

(*Softly.*) They are attempting to build a psychological profile. (*Aloud again.*) You can put either one, 'both', 'neither', or 'don't know'.

AFRA. I'm not sure.

MR TABUTANZER. You're unsure?

AFRA. No. Yes. I mean… yes. I am.

MR TABUTANZER. 'Unsure.' (*Fills in the box and takes up the piece of string.*) Your arm please.

AFRA *offers her arm and he slips the looped string around her wrist, removes it carefully, marking it, and tying a knot, stapling it to the form.*

AFRA. Why did you do that?

MR TABUTANZER. I don't know. Again, it is something from the past. Everything is, you see, in flux. I will also need to take a photo of your teeth. (*Takes a digital camera from his desk drawer.*) Would you please sit under the light?… Thank you… and look up… open please… (*Takes a photo.*) And the top jaw… head back… more… (*Does the same, and checks the image, before popping the camera into the envelope.*) We are nearly there. Last question. Would you swear allegiance to the king?

AFRA. We don't have a king.

MR TABUTANZER. No, we don't, that is right. (*Looks at the next page.*) I see, it continues '… if we had one.' There are three options once again… 'yes', 'no', and 'maybe'?

AFRA. Is this another trap?

MR TABUTANZER. I'm sorry, I can't tell you that. (*Softly.*) Yes.

AFRA (*softly*). What should I say?

MR TABUTANZER (*softly*). Nothing.

AFRA. How…?

MR TABUTANZER. Ssh.

AFRA *nearly speaks, but he indicates for her not to. They wait. After a few moments, the alarm goes off on* MR TABUTANZER*'s digital watch.*

That was close. (*With a big smile.*) We're done.

Contrastingly bright, clear, evocatively exotic music over the short scene change.

Scene Two

The same. AFRA *is sitting almost exactly as before, but is now alone. It is even hotter. She wears a different (but equally sweat-stained) top. The music fades as* MR TABUTANZER *enters briskly, carrying the form.*

MR TABUTANZER. I'm very sorry to have kept you drowning in this solitude. It's extremely excellent to see you again.

A handshake, followed by each wiping their hand.

Please. (*Sitting as well.*) We have good news. I have received back your DV30, and I am delighted to inform you it has been almost unanimously approved. Isn't that fine?

AFRA. Yes. Yes it is.

MR TABUTANZER. There was only one area of concern.

AFRA. Concern?

MR TABUTANZER. I have asked you in, so that we might go through it...

The phone rings.

Do you mind? It is a personal call but this is the only telephone that still works in the present conditions.

AFRA *indicates she doesn't mind.*

(*Into phone.*) Yes. Excuse me, I shall pass you on to him. (*Waiting and then completely de-Africanising his voice.*) Hullo... yes?... Well, they assured me they would... I gave you my credit rating, it was confirmed, we discussed... they called you?... You'll have the confirmation but I'd like to put it on record I think this is appalling! (*Puts phone down, and back to his own voice.*) I am trying to purchase a suit. From a tailor's in London. In tweed. But it seems these days a fellow cannot even buy himself a suit on the expectation of his future fortune without knowing somebody. The banks are out of control! Forgive me raising my voice. Do you know it's three degrees warmer than when you last were here? (*Checks watch*.) However, our fan has been reconditioned. We have a new speed, and between two and four p.m. we can make use of it willy-nilly. Shall we give it a burn?

AFRA *shrugs*. MR TABUTANZER *points a remote control at the fan, which speeds up imperceptibly*.

Brrrr.

AFRA. I wonder… could you stop him staring?

TRUMAN *is glaring at* AFRA *through the blinds*.

MR TABUTANZER. I'm afraid I cannot tell him that because he's not in this office, I'd be stepping on toes. But I can ask, politely. Truman, my friend?

TRUMAN. What?

MR TABUTANZER. I wonder if you would mind not staring at the lady.

TRUMAN. Go to hell. (*Disappears*.)

MR TABUTANZER. Pay no attention to him. He's gone anyway. Let's not allow ourselves to be distracted…

TRUMAN *suddenly runs into the office and aims a vicious-looking blow at* AFRA, *who manages to avoid it, screaming in surprise*. MR TABUTANZER *wrestles* TRUMAN *off and pins his arms*.

There's no call for this at all, my dear fellow…

TRUMAN (*at* AFRA). Maniac!

MR TABUTANZER. Go to lunch! (*Letting* TRUMAN *go*.) Go!

MR TABUTANZER *fetches a handgun from his desk drawer*.

TRUMAN. I'm going… (*At* AFRA.) Snake!

TRUMAN *wags his finger at* AFRA, *almost like a malefaction, and then goes*.

MR TABUTANZER. Ignore him. He has been suffering from personal problems. Someone is sleeping with his wife. Now, let us use this invigorating air and discuss your complaint.

AFRA. There's a difficulty with my complaint?

MR TABUTANZER. No, no, the complaint is proceeding marvellously well. They had just one small concern.

AFRA. Who are 'they'?

MR TABUTANZER. No one. Merely a turn of phrase. All complaints are sent as a matter of course to an independent advisory network, IAN. Ian casts an eye over the preliminary documents and recommends the best course for the complaint to take thereafter, if there's felt to be a problem.

AFRA. So there's a problem...

MR TABUTANZER. No no, not a problem.

AFRA. You said there was.

MR TABUTANZER. *If* there's a problem. There is no problem. Only a concern.

AFRA. A concern is less serious than a problem?

MR TABUTANZER. Many levels less, yes, yes, oh yes. A concern is only one level above the lowest level of all – a slight concern – then there's a concern, and then, ascending from there, an issue, a serious issue, a slight difficulty, and so on up to a problem. Then, confusingly, there's a plain difficulty, which is actually separated from a slight difficulty by a problem. I don't know why it's like that, it just is. But a concern is really very minor indeed.

AFRA. But it's more than a slight concern?

MR TABUTANZER. Yes.

MR TABUTANZER *looks* AFRA *directly in the eye.*

The concern... was not slight. (*Lets the significance sink in.*) That is why I am going to recommend you speak with someone who can help you.

Music, and fast scene change.

Scene Three

The courtyard – a large open space, dramatically half in shadow, its sunny half seeringly bright. AFRA *waits on a backless bench, looking up at the high walls all around her. She turns and stands as she hears* DAWN BIRDCATCHER, *who clips across the ground in noisy heels that echo in the enclosed courtyard. She wears a skirt suit and a fashionable hijab.*

DAWN BIRDCATCHER (*offering her hand*). Dawn Birdcatcher.

    They shake and wipe hands.

    I thought it would be nicer to meet down here in the courtyard. There was a rumour of a breeze… (*Evidently false.*) Shall we sit in the shade? I like to be informal, don't you? It's so much easier to create a *rapport*.

    They sit on the bench, AFRA *conscious of being watched from the windows above and around them. We can just hear the chattering/echoing of voices coming from the windows all around.*

    I remember when shade was something one could feel. It's such a shame, this courtyard's hardly ever used. Don't worry about all the people looking down.

    As AFRA *looks up the echoing/mumbling/chattering of voices around/above them subsides.*

    I'm assuming Mr Tabutanzer explained who I was. Am. I think you're so lucky to have Mr Tabutanzer working on your behalf. Although he's an immigrant to this country he's a very dedicated man. Don't you think so?

AFRA. Yes, very.

DAWN BIRDCATCHER. What?

AFRA. Quite dedicated.

DAWN BIRDCATCHER. 'Quite'? Or 'very'?

> DAWN BIRDCATCHER *produces a form from her briefcase, and is poised to fill out* AFRA*'s answer.*

AFRA. Very.

DAWN BIRDCATCHER (*ticking a box*). I think he's an extraordinary man. Person. Now, let me tell you a bit about me. My name is Dawn Birdcatcher, hello… and I'm the Society's Liaison Advisor. However, you must understand that I don't work for the Society. I'm only attached to the Society. I'm leading on your case for the Society but I'm not *from* the Society.

AFRA. I see. I would like to understand something before we start.

DAWN BIRDCATCHER. Of course you would.

AFRA. You're not from the Society?

DAWN BIRDCATCHER. No.

AFRA. But you report to the Society?

DAWN BIRDCATCHER. Correct.

AFRA. You're independent?

DAWN BIRDCATCHER (*after a moment*). No no no.

AFRA. You must be one or the other.

DAWN BIRDCATCHER. Yes. Or neither. I may be neither. And I'm neither. As Liaison Advisor my function is to advise people, in this instance you, on the best way for the Society to process your complaint.

AFRA. You advise me on the best way for the Society to process my complaint?

DAWN BIRDCATCHER. Yes. I believe Ian had some remarks. (*At her uncertainty.*)…The Independent Advisory Network. Did you read them?

AFRA. I did.

DAWN BIRDCATCHER. You read them?!

AFRA. They were read to me.

DAWN BIRDCATCHER. 'Read to you…' (*Ticking another box.*)

AFRA. By Mr Tabutanzer.

DAWN BIRDCATCHER. Who else! (*Beat.*) I'm asking… (*Her interrogative has been concealed by her exclamation.*) Who else?

AFRA. No one.

She ticks another box, and takes out a little stamping machine, stamps the sheet of paper, tears it off and staples it to the back of the form. As she finishes…

DAWN BIRDCATCHER. Sometimes I don't know what time of day it is. Do you ever have that feeling?

AFRA. Sometimes.

DAWN BIRDCATCHER. How often? Do you have that feeling? How often are you disorientated? The other day I completely forgot where I was. I woke up and looked outside and for about an hour I couldn't say. Everywhere's so like everywhere else, isn't it? Or maybe it's the weather being so interesting. At one moment I was convinced I was in Istanbul, the next it felt like Paris! And then it sort of seeped in I was here. Do you ever get that feeling? Of not knowing where you are?

AFRA. I know where I am.

DAWN BIRDCATCHER. So did I. Do I.

AFRA. I'm not disorientated.

A peel of muffled laughter goes round the courtyard. AFRA *looks up and it stops.*

DAWN BIRDCATCHER. Well, in any case, I'm here to advise you. However, before I advise you, I have to advise you I cannot legally offer you advice.

AFRA. I thought you were the Liaison Advisor?

DAWN BIRDCATCHER. I was. Am. It's confusing, isn't it? Let me explain. I do advise, but only *within* the Society.

AFRA. But you said you didn't work for the Society.

DAWN BIRDCATCHER. Exactly. I don't. I interface between members *of* the Society.

AFRA. Can I ask you another question?

DAWN BIRDCATCHER. No. Not that I can answer. That would be giving advice. I'm here not to advise, but to listen to you, and by listening, assist you in understanding the nature of your concerns.

AFRA. My concerns?

DAWN BIRDCATCHER. Ian's concerns.

AFRA. There was only one, as I understand it. They felt...

DAWN BIRDCATCHER. It. Ian's a network. The Independent Advisory Network. It.

AFRA. It said it felt it didn't feel it knew enough about me, as an individual, and it wanted to get to know me better before assessing the substance of my complaint.

DAWN BIRDCATCHER. Hmnn. I think that's very sensible, don't you? And this is why I'm here, so I can get a sense of what-you-just-said, and take that back to Ian. But first I'm going to tell you a bit about the Society, and its position in the overall ecology. That way everyone gets to know where everyone's coming from. Ecologically. Does that seem like a good idea to you?

AFRA. Fine...

DAWN BIRDCATCHER (*with a form again*). An excellent idea? Or a bad idea?

AFRA. Whichever.

DAWN BIRDCATCHER.... 'Whichever.' (*Ticking another box.*) It's almost like you've seen the form.

There's a hush above. She looks at AFRA, *whose face gives nothing away.*

(*Moving on.*) I want to explain to you how the Society's placed, in reference to itself, apropos its function, especially… and I don't want this to go any further than us… as it approaches its annual review. Going forward. You see, since the reforms, the Society has been in a constant state of self-evaluation. In fact, self-evaluation takes up about ninety per cent of its resources. That's why it's so important they're spent wisely. It just so happens that this time is a very delicate time in the current climate, and by climate I don't mean climate… but this could in fact be the worst possible time for a complaint to be brought against the Society, going forward, at this time.

AFRA. When would be a good time?

DAWN BIRDCATCHER. I can't advise you. Can I just remark that I've really enjoyed listening to you? It's been fascinating and from my point of view very worthwhile. I hope it has been from yours too?

AFRA. Yes…

DAWN BIRDCATCHER. Moderately worthwhile? Or unsatisfactory? (*At* AFRA*'s stare.*) You said 'very' so I'll put that. I'll put very. (*Ticks.*)

She dates the form, folds it, puts it away, stands, and offers her hand.

AFRA (*quietly*). Let's stay in touch.

DAWN BIRDCATCHER. In touch? Yes. Really? What do you mean?

AFRA *smiles, and they shake hands, and wipe.* DAWN BIRDCATCHER *appears a little unnerved, and goes, clip-clopping, exiting after a final look at* AFRA. *The hum of people talking around the walls of the courtyard starts up again.* AFRA *stands for while, looking up at the windows, defiantly. The echoing chatter fades and stops. Music over the scene change.*

Scene Four

The office. MR TABUTANZER *is standing in his T-shirt, having his measurements taken by an irritated* TRUMAN.

TRUMAN. The neck is seventeen!

MR TABUTANZER. Exactly?

TRUMAN. Perhaps you'd like to measure it yourself!

MR TABUTANZER. It cannot be approximate. It must be accurate to a twelfth of an inch. I could be called to the desert at any time...

AFRA *knocks on the jamb of the door, but is unheard by the men. She afterwards enters a step or two into the room and waits.*

TRUMAN. You won't be called, you fool. There's only so far you can rise, you know, even with a tailored suit.

MR TABUTANZER. I could be called imminently... (*Seeing* AFRA, *surprised but covering.*) Oh. Please come in. (*To* TRUMAN.) We'll finish this later.

TRUMAN. I may not be free to do it later.

MR TABUTANZER. You'll do it later.

TRUMAN. You can't make me.

A very short, very untidy scuffle between them that MR TABUTANZER *wins.*

MR TABUTANZER. You trouble your luck, Truman.

TRUMAN. *I* trouble *my* luck!

MR TABUTANZER. Pull yourself together.

TRUMAN. Damn it, she's watching!

Both men glance at the eyes of DAWN BIRDCATCHER
*watching through the blinds. As soon as they look, the blinds
go up, concealing her.*

MR TABUTANZER. Why don't you return to your work.

TRUMAN *straightens himself out and exits (reappearing
moments later in his own office where, during the following,
he pointedly roughly puts up the blinds).*

Tempers are always a little thin when the humidity reaches a
hundred. Can I ask how you managed to find your way past
security?

AFRA. I waited until it was asleep. I'm sorry I didn't make an
appointment. I'm here because I wish to lodge another
complaint. A second complaint.

MR TABUTANZER. I see. Did you not meet with the Liaison
Advisor?

AFRA. It concerns the Liaison Advisor.

MR TABUTANZER *suddenly becomes aware of* TRUMAN
and DAWN BIRDCATCHER *watching again through the
other blinds, which both immediately twitch and close.*

MR TABUTANZER. Your meeting did not go well?

AFRA*'s reaction indicates a negative.* MR TABUTANZER
indicates for AFRA *to take a chair.*

AFRA. At first I didn't understand the purpose of the meeting.
But then it became clear that Miss Birdcatcher's motive was
to try to shanoogle me away from bringing my complaint.

MR TABUTANZER. Shanoogle?

AFRA. Yes.

MR TABUTANZER. That is a very strong word. Please
continue.

AFRA. It seemed to me, rather than to listen to the details of my
complaint, as I had been led to believe was the purpose...

MR TABUTANZER. By who?

AFRA. By you.

MR TABUTANZER. Go on.

AFRA....it seemed in fact to be to morally blackmail me.

ᐧMR TABUTANZER. Morally?

AFRA. Yes.

He gestures for her to wait, closes the door and the last millimetre on the blinds. MR TABUTANZER *takes his seat.*

MR TABUTANZER. Morally? That's the very worst sort. Go on.

AFRA. She told me that my complaint might embarrass the Society in its upcoming spending review.

MR TABUTANZER. Let me get this clear. She told you it might be an inconvenient time for you to bring your complaint?

AFRA. Yes.

MR TABUTANZER. She had no right to say that. And even less right to imply it. I'm going to get to the bottom of this. Please, wait here.

MR TABUTANZER *heads towards the door, then hesitates and goes to his desk and takes out his gun from its drawer.*

Take this. (*Softly.*) Don't worry, it's not loaded. But he doesn't know that. (*Loud.*) It should keep him off if he tries anything. I won't be long. (*Goes.*)

AFRA *settles to wait, immediately disturbed by* TRUMAN *at the blinds. An odd game of peek-a-boo develops. After a while he suddenly appears at a different place, making* AFRA *jump.*

TRUMAN. Hsst.

AFRA. What do you want?

TRUMAN. I don't have a psychological problem.

AFRA. I didn't say you had.

TRUMAN. Yes you did.

After a while.

You don't fool me. I know a subversive when I see one.

After another while…

You think you can slip through the wire. You think because you appear innocent you won't be spotted. But I know what you're doing. You must have planned this minutely. You've got a perfectly plausible reason for everything you say, haven't you? Every gesture. Even your silence.

And another…

I'd like to get hold of you. But we don't do things that way any more. I'll tell you something you ought to know. In here, your friends are your enemies, and your enemies are your friends. Do you know why? Because your enemies sometimes tell you the truth…

TRUMAN *suddenly disappears as the blinds go up, having seen* MR TABUTANZER *coming.*

MR TABUTANZER *enters, looking thoughtful.*

MR TABUTANZER. I don't want to dance around your pond. I shall come straight to the point. I spoke with Miss Birdcatcher, and she told me it was you who raised the matter of the spending review.

AFRA. She told you that?

MR TABUTANZER. She said it was you who raised the subject. Not her.

AFRA. Why would I do that?

MR TABUTANZER. I don't know.

AFRA. Do you believe her?

MR TABUTANZER. This is very awkward.

AFRA. What if I told you I'd recorded our conversation?

MR TABUTANZER. This conversation!?

AFRA. My conversation with Miss Birdcatcher. That I routinely record all conversations with officials, after a frightening childhood experience.

She produces a dictaphone from her bag. MR TABUTANZER *is momentarily knocked off balance.*

MR TABUTANZER. I shall talk again with Miss Birdcatcher.

He goes. TRUMAN *reappears at the blinds.*

TRUMAN. That was clever.

After a while.

I *told* them they were creating a monster.

He waits for a reaction. AFRA*'s face is blank, and then breaks into a smile.* TRUMAN *smiles too.*

But no one listens to me.

He disappears from behind the blinds and seems to reappear magically in the room, holding a large piece of paper and some marker pens.

AFRA. How did you do that?

TRUMAN. A secret door. (*Sticking up the sheet of paper.*)

AFRA. What do you want with me?

TRUMAN. Nothing. Presently. I can deal with you after. I'm going to show you how to bring them down. First you have to know what you're facing. You have no idea what you're facing.

Another stare before TRUMAN *breaks off and starts drawing on the paper to illustrate his points, and every so often running to check the corridor, clearly nervous of* MR TABUTANZER *returning.*

You have to understand the Society is an organism… it's not designed, it has evolved, like coral, a brain… its seat, the seat... of how the information... the sense of its... own... how its fundamental... where the actual... self... itself... whatever you call that... what do you call it?... is in flux... not fixed at all... the individuals inside it are like 'thoughts'... here and gone phhhtt!... there is no soul. And when a thing... anything... like you... attacks... or penetrates... it moves... reorientates itself around you... and consumes you. It can't be defeated. But then there's a problem. Isn't there? With your complaint?

AFRA. Do you think I don't understand how it works? I understand perfectly how it works.

TRUMAN *stares at her for a while, impressed. We hear the faintest hint of* MR TABUTANZER *and* DAWN BIRDCATCHER*'s love-making coming from the other office.* TRUMAN *looks deeply anguished.*

TRUMAN. Now they're doing it in office time. Bastards. This whole place is rotten, rotten. My life is wretched. Stick it to them. That's my advice. Attack attack! If you want to survive. That's all I'm telling you.

We hear giggling from the other office.

That's his leaving-the-room laugh. (*Rapidly taking down the sheet of paper.*)

He scuttles out the way he came. MR TABUTANZER *returns.*

MR TABUTANZER. This is most embarrassing. I don't know what to say... (*Sniffs.*) Was Truman in here?

AFRA *shakes her head.*

I talked again with Miss Birdcatcher. And it appears, that in fact, she never claimed you brought up the matter of the spending review at all.

AFRA. You said she did.

MR TABUTANZER. This is why it's so embarrassing. I misunderstood her. I inferred she had said that you had been the first to mention the spending review, but she hadn't. She never said it at all.

AFRA. Then she admits she was the one who mentioned it?

MR TABUTANZER. I didn't ask her that. I should have asked her, I agree, but my priority was to ensure I understood what she had not said. It may in fact transpire that neither of you said it first.

AFRA. So she didn't deny it wasn't unsaid?

MR TABUTANZER. No, and that's probably how the confusion started. I've taken the precautionary measure of disciplining Miss Birdcatcher if indeed it does transpire otherwise. I've requested she be removed, sideways. (*Takes some paper and starts writing*.) We cannot have this sort of thing going on. We cannot allow your trust to weaken in the Society. For this reason I'm sending you directly to Internal Complaints. They will be able to make an independent assessment of exactly what's been happening. This is a map of how to get from the main entrance to their office. Here's a compass. Count your paces carefully, and head equally north and west. Trust me, this is more reliable than verbal directions. Words can sometimes be ambiguous, don't you think?

He hands her the piece of paper. They shake hands and wipe.

Music over a short scene change, as the screens move and reform into another office, a reverse of MR TABUTANZER*'s, with identical furniture.*

Scene Five

Office. AFRA *enters uncertainly, with the compass. She looks around and sits on one of two chairs. She waits, looking uncertainly and curiously at the office.* DAWN BIRDCATCHER *enters carrying a cardboard box. They both seem surprised to see one another.*

DAWN BIRDCATCHER. You!

AFRA. Yes.

DAWN BIRDCATCHER. How *are* you?

AFRA. Well.

DAWN BIRDCATCHER. It's the devil to find, isn't it?

AFRA. I had a compass.

DAWN BIRDCATCHER. This *is* Internal Complaints?

AFRA. I think so. It seems like I've walked round the whole building.

DAWN BIRDCATCHER. May I sit here?

She takes one of the chairs, using the other, vacated by AFRA, *for her box.*

AFRA. I suppose they wanted to talk to both of us together.

DAWN BIRDCATCHER. Yes. Who?

AFRA. Internal Complaints. I'm sorry you lost your job.

DAWN BIRDCATCHER. Don't think about it. I don't. I never dwell in the past. A bit bare, isn't it?

AFRA. All these offices look the same to me.

DAWN BIRDCATCHER. Yes. It could do with more of a personal touch. I have a plant! (*Takes a cactus out the box.*)

That would look nice there I think.

She hands it to AFRA, *who puts it on the desk.*

That's better. Did they tell you when the interview was going to start?

AFRA. At three.

DAWN BIRDCATCHER. Three. I've actually got something else here that might look right. (*Producing an intray.*) That could be quite useful, couldn't it?

AFRA. I'm sure. Are these from your office?

DAWN BIRDCATCHER. Yes. I was asked to clear my desk.

She brings out another desk object, or piece of stationery.

AFRA. Shouldn't you keep that?

DAWN BIRDCATCHER. What for?

AFRA. Your next job.

DAWN BIRDCATCHER. That's really thinking too far ahead.

She starts to arrange these, and then tips everything, pens, clips, etc., onto the desk.

AFRA. I don't think you should do that. They may not like it.

DAWN BIRDCATCHER. Who?

AFRA. Internal Complaints. The manager.

DAWN BIRDCATCHER *sits at the desk to arrange everything. The truth suddenly sinks in for* AFRA...

It's you! Isn't it? They made you Internal Complaints Manager.

DAWN BIRDCATCHER. Yes.

AFRA. This is...!

DAWN BIRDCATCHER. What?

AFRA. My complaint is against you!

DAWN BIRDCATCHER. That was in a previous life. I assure you, I've checked any personal considerations at that door. I shall be completely impartial.

AFRA. I think this is being done to divert me, because you can't find anything wrong with my complaint.

DAWN BIRDCATCHER. Who told you that?

AFRA. The hysterical man in the office next to Mr Tabutanzer's.

DAWN BIRDCATCHER. That hysterical man, as you put it, is my husband.

AFRA. Truman is your husband?

DAWN BIRDCATCHER. Oh, they call him Truman just to annoy me. Because of his glasses. I know you're wondering why I married him. When I met him he was a different man entirely. They thought he would even make Prosecutor. I was one of his… clients. I can still remember the feeling when he cross-examined me. He was so dynamic, I was completely in awe of him. Well, everyone was. I became his secretary, after. You see, he was the victim of his own success. No one dared cross him, and so the work dropped off. I retrained as a liaison advisor. And then Mr Tabutanzer moved in to the office between us. It's all your fault. If it hadn't been for your complaint, nothing would've happened. The excitement when it first came in… the shock… it was all so… alive. There would have been no late nights poring over the paperwork. If I'm thrown out, I won't be able to bear it. Do you think an administrator's heart doesn't beat? That the world doesn't exist beyond your silly complaint? That we aren't human?

There is a silence and then AFRA *starts laughing.* DAWN BIRDCATCHER *watches her.*

Don't pretend you don't find this baffling. You do. Say you do!

AFRA. Yes yes. If you like. (*After recovering.*) How do we go about this?

DAWN BIRDCATCHER. You must register your secondary complaint.

After drying her eyes AFRA *takes a deep metaphorical breath…*

AFRA. Very well. I wish to lodge a secondary complaint…

DAWN BIRDCATCHER. Against?

AFRA. The Liaison Advisor.

DAWN BIRDCATCHER. I'm filling in her name. (*Writing.*) Can I ask the grounds?

AFRA. She attempted to morally blackmail me.

DAWN BIRDCATCHER. Morally? (*Tuts.*) That's the worse sort, isn't it? How did that make you feel? I bet you were *furious*. Out of control even. Were you? And you'd have every right to be. And she definitely said that?

AFRA. Yes.

DAWN BIRDCATCHER. It infuriates *me*, and I'm not you.

AFRA. It won't work, you know.

DAWN BIRDCATCHER. What…?

AFRA. This. If you think this will drive me crazy, you're wrong.

DAWN BIRDCATCHER. I don't understand. You find my demeanour too professional?

AFRA. Just tell me. What will happen to my complaint?

DAWN BIRDCATCHER. This one or the original…?

AFRA. *This* one.

DAWN BIRDCATCHER. It depends on whether you want to take it further. Of course, it will have to be resolved prior to the processing of your original complaint, because it directly calls into question the personnel involved. Me. Her. Us. We're the personnel. So there'll be a delay.

AFRA. How long a delay?

DAWN BIRDCATCHER. About two weeks. A year.

AFRA. Then I wish to make a third complaint.

DAWN BIRDCATCHER (*after the shock*). A third…? A third.
(*Flustered.*) Of course. But you'll need to make an
appointment.

She picks up the desk phone and pulls its wire from the wall.

At reception. This isn't connected. Why are you laughing? It
isn't funny at all. From your point of view, it's very
frustrating.

AFRA *offers her hand. They shake, and wipe.* AFRA *leaves,
smiling.* DAWN BIRDCATCHER *goes to the door, and
checks she has gone, looking up and down the corridor,
unnerved, returns and picks up the phone to make a call,
realising it isn't working.*

*Music over – lengthy, and with a break in the middle,
suggesting a passage of time.*

Scene Six

MR TABUTANZER*'s office.* MR TABUTANZER, *in a very
sharp, tailored tweed suit, scarf and gloves, is opening a bottle
of champagne.* TRUMAN, *in coat and gloves, is holding a large
plant under one arm and a mysterious little machine in the other.
He is smiling, and appears transformed, even radiant. It is
clearly very cold. The champagne pops.* AFRA *enters, wearing
a sand-encrusted coat, as* MR TABUTANZER *pours the
champagne into an improvised assortment of cups and glasses.*

MR TABUTANZER. Come in, come in!

AFRA. I'm sorry…

MR TABUTANZER. Please!

AFRA. I didn't mean to interrupt...

MR TABUTANZER. No no, join us! We are celebrating good news. I am so sorry it has taken so long to find you an appointment.

AFRA. Four months.

MR TABUTANZER. Is it? Was it? Has it been so long?

AFRA. Four months.

MR TABUTANZER. Four months. Well, we've been so busy. And so much has changed. The pace of reform. You know on average your waiting time, aggregated and divided by your number of appointments overall has been only three weeks, which complies comfortably with our waiting-time target.

AFRA. Is this celebration connected to my complaint?

MR TABUTANZER. It is, indeed, indeed connected. To your complaint. How did you know that?

AFRA *shrugs, inscrutably.* MR TABUTANZER *whispers something to* TRUMAN, *who makes a very short, silent call on the phone.*

I can tell you, very happily, that because of the most unsatisfactory way this department has handled your complaint, that we are to receive a massive increase in funding.

TRUMAN. It's a great vote of confidence in the future of the department.

MR TABUTANZER. I myself am personally being sent to a secret desert location to be retrained. I am to have my management practices upgraded with the most recent techniques from abroad. All in all, therefore, I can say everything has worked out marvellously well.

They respond and drink. The sound of a horn outside.

My bus. (*Dressing in his coat and hat, etc*.) In my absence a special report has been commissioned, that will look into every aspect of the department's activities. Truman here has been appointed to deliver it. I shall leave you in his capable hands. (*Softly*.) He's a completely different man. (*Loud*.) Farewell.

He takes his gloves and leaves. As he does so he has to squeeze past a black leather armchair entering in front of a COURIER *covered in sand, with his face and body wrapped in a sand-encrusted scarf.*

TRUMAN. My chair!

The COURIER (*played by the actor playing* DAWN BIRDCATCHER*) puts it down, and locates her pen and ledger.* TRUMAN *runs the machine he has been carrying slowly over the surface of the chair. It emits the odd, intermittent distinctive crackle of a Geiger counter. He then runs it over the* COURIER. *It gives off the same crackle before a more constant noise as it reaches the* COURIER*'s shoes.*

(*Reads dial.*) I'd move those on if I were you.

The COURIER *grunts and hands* TRUMAN *the ledger to sign.* TRUMAN *signs it and the* COURIER *leaves. After a moment...*

AFRA. You seem a happier man.

TRUMAN. I am... refulgent. I don't know if that's a word but it sums up my state of being precisely. My life has been entirely turned around. How fast things move these days. Would you like to share my picnic?

AFRA. I've eaten.

TRUMAN. Let me tempt you. I have farki and some chermoula. There's even some mergueza, done in the American manner, with pickles, cheese, and ketchup, in a sesame bun.

AFRA (*unable to conceal her hunger*). Perhaps some chermoula.

TRUMAN. And the best part of it all? Not only has *he* been sent away, but my wife has been given a year's contract to investigate herself. She has moved into my old office.

The blinds twitch and close.

So, it really has turned out remarkably well. Thanks to you. (*Softly.*) She's upset he's gone, of course, but that's my opportunity, isn't it? To win her back. (*Aloud.*) So. Here we are. (*Produces a sterilised, wrapped pen and offers it from its wrapper.*) You need to sign this.

AFRA. What is it?

TRUMAN. It permits you to use the gymnasium, and facilities, for overnight stays, the cafeteria, showers, locker area, et cetera. They're very generous in that way. Just there. And there. Don't touch the paper! Thank you. (*Disposes of the pen, and indicates the chair.*) Please. (*Indicating the chair.*)

AFRA. Before we proceed, can I ask you a question?

TRUMAN. No.

AFRA. What?

TRUMAN. I'm sorry, I was too quick. Ask what? Of course.

AFRA. What has happened to my complaint?

TRUMAN. In what sense?

AFRA. Where is it?

TRUMAN. Where?

AFRA. In the process. What has happened to it in these four months?

TRUMAN. I see, in that sense. Your complaint has been upheld.

AFRA. Upheld?

TRUMAN. Indeed.

AFRA. By who?

TRUMAN. The Complaints Review Committee.

AFRA. When did that happen?

TRUMAN. Tomorrow.

AFRA. They upheld it tomorrow?

TRUMAN. No. That would make no sense at all. They will meet tomorrow. But in order to meet they first had to uphold the complaint.

AFRA. Shouldn't they have met before they upheld it?

TRUMAN. You'd have thought so, wouldn't you? But this report couldn't have gone ahead unless your complaint was acknowledged. Of course by 'upheld', I mean it has only been temporarily upheld. What goes up must come down. It would be more accurate to say your complaint has been suspended.

AFRA. Suspended?

TRUMAN. But only indefinitely.

AFRA (*after a while*). I'd like to ask something else.

TRUMAN. Please.

AFRA. It's something that's concerned me since I first approached the Society with my complaint.

TRUMAN. Yes?

AFRA. I still haven't stated what it is.

TRUMAN. The complaint?

AFRA. No.

TRUMAN. And that's why it's got as far as it has. That's why it's been taken so seriously. That's why everyone's been running round in circles. That's been its genius. Its devastating and unanswerable quality. Will you also read this please and sign?

AFRA. What is it?

TRUMAN. It permits the use of restraints. If you're not interrogated properly it won't look good in the report. It will help the process enormously. Restraints will make you feel less secure and this will allow your resistance to be thoroughly tested...

AFRA. You don't need to persuade me. (*Signing.*) I quite understand.

TRUMAN (*uneasily*). You do?

AFRA. Yes. Now you'll be able to detect any fault lines.

TRUMAN *looks a little troubled, and presses the arms of the chair. Restraints appear. He clips these over* AFRA's *wrists.*

TRUMAN. Do you feel less secure?

AFRA. Yes. That's much better. What's the matter?

TRUMAN *stands, suddenly staring into the distance, distracted. He lets out a long sigh.*

TRUMAN. It's brought back happier times. (*Snapping out of it.*) In the old days you'd be black and blue, you know, already, and I could go to town on you... without filling out A COLUMN OF PAPERWORK!

AFRA. I'm sorry. Really I am.

TRUMAN. It's not your fault. It's not your fault. The world is simply out of control.

Music, very briefly, over a rapid scene change.

Scene Seven

The same – but later. It is now evidently very cold. Both are dressed in improvised cold-weather gear, including gloves, overcoats, furs, and improvised headgear. TRUMAN *is in the middle of some very impassioned questioning…*

TRUMAN. Why are you terrorising our Society?

AFRA. I'm not.

TRUMAN. Is your plan to bring the whole edifice down about your ears?

AFRA. No.

TRUMAN. Then what are you doing here?

AFRA. Only seeing through my complaint.

TRUMAN. So you say. (*Taking a breather.*) Your life seems to have been designed to cause trouble. Everything you've done seems to have been for that purpose. And this is a coincidence?

AFRA. Yes.

TRUMAN (*after a while*). Tell me again, what you say you do?

AFRA. Nothing.

TRUMAN. Where? Do you do it?

AFRA. Anywhere.

TRUMAN. I shall tell you what you do, and you can agree, or disagree. You stand. Don't you?

AFRA. Sometimes.

TRUMAN. And sit.

AFRA. Occasionally.

TRUMAN. And sometimes you walk? And now and then you'll dress in provocative clothing.

AFRA. I have never worn anything deliberately provocative.

TRUMAN. Once you stood in the square with a question mark on your back.

AFRA. It was a scarf.

TRUMAN. In the shape of a question mark.

AFRA. So I was told.

TRUMAN. You don't deny it then?

AFRA. It was just the way the material fell.

TRUMAN. You like to stand, don't you? Very still.

AFRA. Yes, we established that.

TRUMAN. And walk.

AFRA. Daily.

TRUMAN. But not in the way that others stand, or walk.

AFRA. I don't know what you mean.

TRUMAN. Tell me about the plinth. You stand on. In the square.

AFRA. Is that what it is?

TRUMAN. Why do you do it?

AFRA. To get a view.

TRUMAN. Of what? What are you looking at? When you stand on your plinth.

AFRA. It isn't *my* plinth. It's just there.

TRUMAN. Nevertheless, some refer to it as your plinth.

AFRA. Do they?

TRUMAN. You've stood on that plinth on over twenty separate occasions.

AFRA. Have I really?

TRUMAN. Staring.

AFRA. At what?

TRUMAN. The buildings. Whose buildings are they in the square?

AFRA. They belong to the Society.

TRUMAN. Has it crossed your mind that by standing as you do, regularly, on a plinth in President King Square, and staring at the buildings, you might be drawing attention to yourself?

AFRA. I hadn't thought of that.

TRUMAN suddenly inexplicably exits. We hear a mosque some distance away calling to prayer. TRUMAN returns with a small machine. This he puts on the desk and starts to attach to two small bars.

What's that…?

TRUMAN. It's a polygraph.

AFRA. A lie-detector?

TRUMAN. You don't mind?

AFRA. No. Of course I don't mind.

TRUMAN. Why should you?

AFRA. I don't mind at all.

TRUMAN. You hold these here, and here… squeeze tightly… and I tape around your fists, like this… clench… and like this… again… and there we are. Is that comfortable?

AFRA. No, not 'comfortable'.

TRUMAN. They should be moderately uncomfortable. Now I have to adjust the settings. To do this I will ask you some questions. I'd like you to listen, count to three, and then answer 'yes' to each question. Are you ready?

Pause.

AFRA. Yes.

TRUMAN. I haven't started yet. You didn't have to pause. I shall start now.

Are you sitting on a chair?

Pause.

AFRA. Yes.

TRUMAN. Are you a female?

Pause.

AFRA. Yes.

TRUMAN. Are you apprehensive?

AFRA. No. I mean... (*Pause.*) yes.

TRUMAN. Are you sitting on a chair?

Pause.

AFRA. Yes.

TRUMAN. Are you the Emperor of China?

Pause.

AFRA. Yes.

TRUMAN. Now we can begin. Take your time. Think very hard about the questions, and answer each one truthfully. Are you an artist?

AFRA. No.

TRUMAN *checks the polygraph again, and then looks at his file.*

TRUMAN. So it seems. Or at least you don't consider yourself to be an artist. On one occasion standing on your plinth, however, you sang. Didn't you? A foreign song. Do you remember what it was?

AFRA. No.

TRUMAN *checks the polygraph.*

TRUMAN. Tell me about the sign.

AFRA. I don't know what you mean.

TRUMAN. A wooden sign. About so big. It was placed against your plinth.

AFRA. This is the first time I've heard about it.

TRUMAN. So someone else put it there?

AFRA. Did they?

TRUMAN. A confederate. (*Here as elsewhere checking the polygraph.*)

AFRA. I don't know anything about it.

TRUMAN. Are you saying you were not aware of the sign? That whoever put it there was entirely unknown to you?

AFRA. Yes.

TRUMAN (*after checking the polygraph*). Apparently so.

AFRA. What did it say? The sign?

TRUMAN. It was blank. Which could be seen as quite incendiary. It was on the day the policeman approached you. You remember him?

AFRA. No.

TRUMAN. He was plain clothes. You remember now? What did he say?

AFRA. He asked me about the sign.

TRUMAN. But when I asked you about the sign, you said you didn't remember it.

AFRA. That's right. I've always wondered what the man meant when he asked me about 'a sign'. And only now it makes sense.

TRUMAN. Can I believe you?

AFRA. Yes.

TRUMAN (*after checking the polygraph again, a little confused*). Apparently so. I can. Did. How did the conversation proceed with the policeman?

AFRA. There wasn't really a conversation. I didn't answer him. I didn't know he was a policeman. I thought he was just a creep, being mysterious. Talking about 'a sign'.

TRUMAN. He didn't tell you he was a policeman?

AFRA. No. If he had I would happily have entered into conversation.

TRUMAN. Would you?

AFRA. Yes. How am I doing?

TRUMAN (*after studying the polygraph*). Very well. In fact perfectly. Which is suspicious. (*Brings out a form and puts it in front of* AFRA.)

Will you sign this?

AFRA. What is it?

TRUMAN. An assent form for receiving shocks through the polygraph.

AFRA. Electrical shocks?

TRUMAN. It's a little adaptation I made to the polygraph. I discovered if there's the threat of an electric charge a polygraph becomes almost completely reliable. So it's very much in your interest. I can't electrocute you unless you agree. Because of these ABSURD reforms!

AFRA (*reading the assent form*). Five hundred volts?

TRUMAN. Up to. I'll never actually administer that level. That's just a legal cover. In case.

AFRA. Of what?

TRUMAN. An accident.

AFRA. Reach in my pocket.

TRUMAN (*after some effort and trouble, producing a sheath of papers*). What is this?

AFRA. The same agreement, signed before my own witnesses.

TRUMAN *flicks through and sees this is the case.*

TRUMAN. You came prepared.

AFRA. I always carry a copy. Since an unfortunate childhood experience.

TRUMAN *pockets this, and fits two wires to the machine, and charges it by its dynamo wheel.*

TRUMAN. Shall we give it a try? This will be just beneath the legal limit. This is to help you, you understand? Otherwise you won't know what to expect if you lie.

He does so. It is clearly extremely painful. AFRA *is left recovering for a while.*

Too much?

AFRA. No. That seemed about right.

TRUMAN, *expecting a stronger reaction, is knocked off his stride. He covers and busies himself with his notes. Music, over –*

Scene Eight

A basement. AFRA *is lying on the floor in a pool of light on a mattress. A heavy door opens and* DAWN BIRDCATCHER *(dressed in cheap but thick furs) enters with a tray. She puts it on the floor, and pours two cups of tea from a height, from a long-spouted silver teapot,*

DAWN BIRDCATCHER. I thought you might like tea. When I saw you were an overnight I switched my roster. I'm a volunteer. I'm afraid it's rather basic down here. I hope you take sugar.

AFRA *slowly sits up, teeth chattering, grateful for the hot drink.*

It's quite a process, isn't it? In other countries this sort of thing is left entirely to the courtroom. It's just sprung on you and it's the luck of the dice, frankly, how you come out of it. I think this is a much better way. Far better to be cross-examined by a sympathetic ear. It's such a good thing for Truman too. Listening to him going at you through the wall... I have to admit something did stir in me again. He's been dreaming of something like this that he could really get his teeth into. I'm physically so attracted to Mr Tabutanzer. He's absolutely my type. I find a strong-willed man irresistible. He's the sort of man you could bite. He was Truman's junior, but he shot past him on the reforming wind. Everything's been in such a... flux. One day they altered all the light fittings, practically overnight. I'm so admiring of what you're doing, taking on the Society like this, so brave. Sacrificing yourself. It must be hard to maintain the mask.

AFRA. Do you mind if I don't speak?

DAWN BIRDCATCHER. Not at all. They ought to have given you an extra blanket. You should complain. A fourth complaint! Did you know your third would trigger a report? You must have known? Did you? Who told you? An insider?

AFRA *is clearly not going to say a word.*

Things are moving so fast. There's so much changed about the Society even since you came here. (*After another silence.*) I'm so unhappy you mistrust me. It makes me so sad. I don't know why we never became friends. Is it because of our previous misunderstandings?

The door-slot-opening sound, light thrown in. And closes again.

It's nice they look in every now and then.

AFRA. I intend to see through my complaint.

They drink tea for a while in silence.

DAWN BIRDCATCHER. Yes. I'm going to go.

She suddenly takes up the tea things and goes. Music, over –

Scene Nine

The office again, still cold but no longer freezing. TRUMAN *enters in a coat but removes this to reveal a faux-leather jacket, shirt, polyester slacks and leather shoes. He does his tie in a mirror. He barely looks at* AFRA *who has entered, sat, taken up the polygraph/shock bars, and is putting the tape around her hands, ultimately with her teeth. When* TRUMAN *finishes with his tie he consults the file on his desk, very much the lawyer in control, before approaching* AFRA.

TRUMAN. Once more. Are you an artist?

AFRA. No.

TRUMAN. Are you an artist?

AFRA. No.

TRUMAN *checks the polygraph.*

TRUMAN. It's remarkable.

AFRA. What is?

TRUMAN. Your ability to go undetected by a polygraph. Your ability to keep your biorhythms level. It may be evidence against you. Have you acquired an advanced meditative capacity? Perhaps it's a skill you developed standing so long on your plinth.

AFRA. I don't understand your question.

TRUMAN. Is it why you've been chosen to lead this attack on our Society?

AFRA. I don't think I've been chosen for anything.

TRUMAN. Do you know you were shot at?

AFRA. Shot at?

TRUMAN. Yes.

AFRA. By whom?

TRUMAN. It was never discovered. The investigation calculated it must have come from a window on the north side of the square, passed very, very close to your ear and travelled down President King Avenue – A child playing in the street was hit by the bullet half a kilometre away.

AFRA. Let me think… When did this happen?

TRUMAN. The beginning of October. You don't remember?
`   You don't recall a bullet whistling past your ear one morning, at about 9.40 a.m?

AFRA. No.

TRUMAN. Possibly taking a little nick? (*Close to her, inspecting her ear.*)

AFRA. I do remember that!

TRUMAN. Now you do?

AFRA. I thought it was an insect bite. I thought it was odd at the time... (*Screams from an electric shock.*)

TRUMAN. There was a small variation of the needle on your answer. Just on the line. It may have been caused by ironic understatement.

AFRA (*recovering*)....Shit... shit...

TRUMAN *consults his file, taking his time as* AFRA *recovers.*

TRUMAN. When you were arrested...

AFRA. I've never been arrested.

TRUMAN. When you were escorted from President King Square, what were you doing?

AFRA. I was standing.

TRUMAN. On your plinth, yes, and what happened? Someone approached you. Who?

AFRA. I don't know.

TRUMAN. Another policeman?

AFRA. No. The person wore a sort of skirt.

TRUMAN. A woman?

AFRA. Yes, that would explain it perfectly.

TRUMAN (*at the polygraph*). That was very close. Who was she?

AFRA. She told me she was a member of the Society...

TRUMAN. And...

AFRA. She asked me to walk with her.

TRUMAN. Politely?

AFRA. Exquisitely.

TRUMAN. What did you do?

AFRA. The first time? I went along.

TRUMAN. Where to?

AFRA. The river.

TRUMAN. And what did she tell you there?

AFRA. She told me if I went back to the square I would be arrested.

TRUMAN. She was giving you information. Assisting you?

AFRA. Yes, I suppose she was.

TRUMAN. And this happened again. According to this file you were asked to move on on no less than ten occasions. On each occasion you were standing, walking or sitting in a public place in a way that could be described as 'expressive'. (*Really taking his time and observing* AFRA *for a crack in her defences.*) That is why I ask again if you're an artist. If you are we can end this here and now.

AFRA. Was that you asking?

TRUMAN. Yes.

AFRA. I am not. An artist.

TRUMAN. The reason I ask if you're an artist is because, as you know, if you were you would have a licence to be expressive. But you're wise to deny it, because, as you also know, it is illegal to be a public artist without a licence.

AFRA. I don't agree I was behaving in a way that was 'expressive'. And I would ask you, with some curiosity, to say what you mean by 'artist'.

TRUMAN. I shall. I googled – (*Pronouncing like 'good'.*) the word to discover what it meant.

AFRA. Googled?

TRUMAN. Yes, googled. It's a word. (*Reads.*) 'Art can be said to occur when a person is aware of looking at something of interest. (*Scrolling on.*) Art also takes place when a person is conscious of being observed, or produces, or intends to produce, an object or event with that purpose. (*Scrolling.*) A person alone in their home, or among family, goes largely unobserved, and that is why such people must leave the home in order to commit art.'

AFRA. That's an interesting definition.

TRUMAN. It's from an article by an eminent French criminologist. Now, if you are not an artist and you do not wish to be observed, what is your reason for doing what you do in public places?

AFRA. No reason.

TRUMAN. You are not aware of being observed?

AFRA. Who by?

TRUMAN. The… Society. (*After a moment.*) Now, don't you see your position is altered? Now that you know you're being observed, you face the extremely serious charge of being a self-appointed artist.

AFRA. But no one's looking at me, here. Apart from Miss Birdcatcher.

TRUMAN. But they are! They are looking at you by your absence.

AFRA. Who are?

TRUMAN. Well, for a start, the many thousands of people who follow your activities on their 'social media'!

AFRA *looks astonished.*

You had no idea?

AFRA. No.

TRUMAN (*checking the polygraph*). Indeed you did not, you did not. (*Flaring.*) How are you managing to do this? You are unaware that each day you remain in this building these people… (*Checking his notes.*) 'Twitter' for your release? That you are a focus of this activity?

AFRA. I'm sorry, I thought you'd become rhetorical. What did you ask me?

TRUMAN. Are you in a dream? Is that the trick? Have you hypnotised yourself? Have you persuaded yourself the world is a dream? That there are no such things as lies, or truth, that one thing is unconnected to another in any causal way? Is that how you're able to lie so undetectably?

AFRA. I really couldn't tell you.

TRUMAN. What happened on the tenth time you were escorted from the square?

AFRA. I don't remember.

TRUMAN. Something happened.

AFRA. Did it?

TRUMAN. There were two men.

AFRA. Really?

TRUMAN. They drove you away.

AFRA. What did they do?

TRUMAN. You tell me. You tell me.

AFRA (*after a long silence*). I don't remember.

TRUMAN (*after checking the polygraph closely*). No you don't. What's the point of this apparatus?

He tears off the wires and taping around her hands.

The problem with your complaint, as I have explained, is that there is no problem with it because you haven't made it. And if that's the case we have a very great difficulty. Because no one's to blame. And if there's no one to blame, then everyone has acted correctly. And if everyone has acted correctly then it can only be the Society at fault...

AFRA....which is impossible.

After a moment he grabs her. She does not react.

TRUMAN. You don't seem to understand your innocence is forcing this Society to go on the offensive.

He pushes her away, takes the phone and presses a number.

AFRA. Who are you calling?

TRUMAN. Internal Complaints. (*Shakes the phone.*) Damn this infernal moon! (*Slams it down.*) Excuse me… (*Goes to the blinds.*) The phone isn't working, would you come in here, please.

DAWN BIRDCATCHER (*from the other side of the blinds*). Certainly.

TRUMAN *goes to the desk again, rummages and brings out some extra-large headphones with a small old-fashioned cassette recorder.*

TRUMAN. Please put these on.

AFRA. What are they for?

TRUMAN. So you can't hear what we're saying. We're obliged to… the reforms. Which music do you prefer? Classical or modern?

AFRA. Modern.

TRUMAN. Are you sure? Some of it was quite avant-garde.

AFRA. I'm very open-minded.

AFRA *puts on the headphones.* DAWN BIRDCATCHER *enters. She and* AFRA *mouth 'hello' at one another.* TRUMAN *guides* DAWN BIRDCATCHER *forward to talk discreetly. They check* AFRA *is occupied by the music, and feel confident that she is by her growingly confused expression.*

DAWN BIRDCATCHER. Why did you stop?

TRUMAN. I can't get anywhere with her.

DAWN BIRDCATCHER. But you were doing so marvellously, I was listening…

TRUMAN. We have to dispose of her.

DAWN BIRDCATCHER. What do you mean?

TRUMAN. Get rid of her for me.

DAWN BIRDCATCHER. I'm not your mother.

TRUMAN. What are you talking about? My mother would never get rid of someone for me, even if I begged her.

DAWN BIRDCATCHER. Then I don't see why I should.

TRUMAN. Why don't you just admit you have stronger feelings for *him* than you do for me?

DAWN BIRDCATCHER. Don't keep bringing him into this. My feelings for Mr Tabutanzer are stronger, yes, but they're not as complicated. I'm not doing your dirty laundry.

TRUMAN. I'm not asking you to do my laundry personally, just arrange for it to be done. By launderers. I can't! I'm meant to be writing a balanced report and it would be a serious breach of professional detachment to be involved.

DAWN BIRDCATCHER. I don't even know where one would find a person to do such a thing.

TRUMAN. The phone book, shitwit.

DAWN BIRDCATCHER. Don't be so nasty.

TRUMAN. I'm sorry. I'm finding this… balance… very stressful.

DAWN BIRDCATCHER. Oh, Truman, you haven't changed at all.

TRUMAN. That's a terrible thing to say. I have changed.

DAWN BIRDCATCHER. Well, it doesn't feel like it.

TRUMAN. Just do it. And make sure the killer's… good.

She goes. TRUMAN *watches* AFRA, *who has taken off her earphones and is watching him with a smile.* TRUMAN *stares back, unnerved.*

Music, over –

Scene Ten

The same – with TRUMAN *and* AFRA *sitting completely inanimately, waiting. Enter* DAWN BIRDCATCHER, *followed by a man dressed as a Tuareg (the actor playing* MR TABUTANZER), *in tribal robes of spotlessly clean, deepest, brightest, royal blue. Wrapped round his head, face and shoulders is a headdress of the same colour. He has a pair of reflective shades so that only his hands and a sliver of cheek are visible. A very deadly and non-ornamental-looking knife hangs from his belt in a scabbard.* TRUMAN, *slightly nervously, gestures him towards one of the wooden chairs, placed in a dark corner.* TRUMAN *brings* DAWN BIRDCATCHER *forward. They talk softly, while* AFRA *looks at the Tuareg, with curiosity.*

TRUMAN. This is him?

DAWN BIRDCATCHER. Yes.

TRUMAN. How did you find him?

DAWN BIRDCATCHER. He was recommended.

TRUMAN. He's unusually dressed.

DAWN BIRDCATCHER. He's a Tuareg. It's not unusual for him.

TRUMAN. Is he discreet?

DAWN BIRDCATCHER. I don't know. No one speaks Tuareg. I suppose that would make him discreet. I don't want to be here when... you know.

TRUMAN. We'll be a very, very long way away, somewhere there'll be plenty of witnesses.

DAWN BIRDCATCHER. Oh, darling. You're yourself again.

AFRA. Who's this?

TRUMAN and DAWN BIRDCATCHER *part.* TRUMAN
goes to his desk where a form has been placed.

TRUMAN. Please don't be alarmed. Our friend is here to help
us. We only need to fill this out and we can bring all this to a
conclusion.

AFRA. What's this?

TRUMAN. A statement that there's been a complaint, and that
it's been dealt with, and everyone has acted correctly, and
you haven't felt under any threat, personally, or pressure...

AFRA. Threat?

TRUMAN. Yes, it's rather silly, formal language, but it's
necessary I'm afraid. A sort of indemnity, stating in the event
of disappearance, that you, or your relatives, absolve the
Society from any blame, and you understand and accept the
reasons for your disappearance. And at the bottom is a little
clause apologising for embarrassment or expense to the
Society. And that's it. All quite standard. Ridiculous really,
but they brought it in during the reforms, and we're obliged...

AFRA. You mean to kill me?

TRUMAN. Dispose of you. That could mean a range of things.
Only in this case does it have that connotation, yes, to be
fair, it does.

DAWN BIRDCATCHER. She's upset. Is it the prospect of
extinction?

AFRA. No no, I'm not upset at all. It's just been such a long...

DAWN BIRDCATCHER. She's not upset.

AFRA....a long... road. I'm quite prepared.

TRUMAN. And that's our point. To be prepared. You ought to
think of your family. Their standing in the community. The
statement clears them of any complicity. Which I'm sure will
be an important consideration. And there's also a generous
financial package. A pension scheme. Final salary linked.

He puts the form before AFRA*'s eyes.*

The fruit of the reforms. It may seem morbid to you now but if you think about it unselfishly…

AFRA. No, of course. One doesn't think of these things. I'm very happy to sign, but can you tell me a bit more? Is this the best possible scheme?

TRUMAN. No, we're not allowed to advise.

MR TABUTANZER. Stop! There!

The Tuareg takes off his shades with a flourish and reveals himself as MR TABUTANZER.

It is I.

DAWN BIRDCATCHER. Mr Tabutanzer! (*To* TRUMAN.) I had no idea, really…

MR TABUTANZER. She didn't know.

TRUMAN *is speechless, turning to* DAWN BIRDCATCHER *for an explanation.*

DAWN BIRDCATCHER. I looked in the phone book but I couldn't pluck up the nerve, so I rang Mr Tabutanzer. He said he'd arrange it, and when this man arrived in his desert robes, I thought Mr Tabutanzer had sent him.

MR TABUTANZER. A smart disguise, no? Purchased, I must tell you, from the airport shop, for one hundred and ninety-nine dollars. I thought it might do also for weddings and occasions. It is a most providential thing for all of us that I am returned, and just in time, I think, to persuade you things do not have to be the way they are! I come from the wilderness, where I attended a great meeting of our people from the four corners of the world. In that desert, in that great silence, we ideated, one administrator to another, and we listened to the Speaker. I shall take you to a place such as I have been, a higher place, beneath the stars. There is such a place, even here, in the city, in this building! Or rather above. Let us go to the roof! Where the setting sun now stirs the summer wind. We shall sit together as I did at the gathering in the desert, and I shall tell you the message we received. Bring her! – (*At* AFRA.) gagged and tied to a chair. Greet those you meet in the corridors with a smile, and if they ask you why you're carrying a woman tied to a chair, say we're rehearsing for a Jewish wedding.

DAWN BIRDCATCHER. You've thought of everything.

He sweeps out laughing, in agreement. As they tie AFRA *to a wooden chair –*

TRUMAN. You've broken my heart, a second time.

DAWN BIRDCATCHER. I didn't know who else to turn to.

TRUMAN. I shan't trust you again.

DAWN BIRDCATCHER. I didn't know he'd come himself.

TRUMAN. He's gone insane. Can't you see the look in his eye?

DAWN BIRDCATCHER. Do you think?

TRUMAN. He's had some sort of religious conversion.

DAWN BIRDCATCHER. Now I'm worried.

As they go, carrying out AFRA *in the chair –*

I'm sorry... I'm sorry...

TRUMAN. You're sorry...!

Fading as they go.

DAWN BIRDCATCHER. Assassination is new territory for me...

TRUMAN. You didn't even discuss the details...?

DAWN BIRDCATCHER. You think I knew it was him!... don't you...

TRUMAN. I didn't say that...

DAWN BIRDCATCHER. But you do...

Music, over –

Scene Eleven

The roof. Behind, the sky is a deep, late-evening blue, with the very first stars just emerging. The blinds have become roof ventilation covers, and other city roofs are visible around and in the distance. It is still cold. MR TABUTANZER *stares out over the skyline, in his robes, as* DAWN BIRDCATCHER *and* TRUMAN *drag* AFRA *onto the roof in the chair.* DAWN BIRDCATCHER *recovers from the exertion as* TRUMAN *goes directly to* MR TABUTANZER.

TRUMAN. Why don't we just tip her into the courtyard while we can. We're dealing here with a new and most dangerous type of subversion. The innocent subversive. But these people must be met with in the same old way.

MR TABUTANZER. With violence?

TRUMAN. It is the humane response. Yes, a little plain and honest violence. At least it has some flesh and blood about it.

A distant rumble. They all turn and look at the smoke on the horizon.

You see that? Smoke. Fear is how government's been done since men were apes. The snarl, the bark, the sudden decisive blow. This has been the way of sound administration since time began.

MR TABUTANZER. I say no.

TRUMAN. I know what you're bringing from your 'holy gathering' in the desert. And it's madness.

MR TABUTANZER. I bring the future.

TRUMAN grabs the chair containing AFRA and hauls it towards the edge of the roof.

DAWN BIRDCATCHER. What are you doing!?

There is a struggle over the chair, and the gagged AFRA.
MR TABUTANZER *watches, untroubled.*

TRUMAN. We must act now…

DAWN BIRDCATCHER. Stop!

TRUMAN.…while we can!

*The struggle continues with the chair tipping forward over
the edge. Only the ropes, holding* AFRA*'s arms, prevent her
from falling into the courtyard.*

DAWN BIRDCATCHER. No!

TRUMAN. This is what we're paid for! And if there are no men
left prepared to do these things then civilisation is finished!

He shrugs her off and tips the chair and AFRA *forward as
far as he can, but then hesitates.*

DAWN BIRDCATCHER. Oh, Truman.

TRUMAN. I haven't lost my nerve. It's just this damned
innocence.

He brings the chair back to the vertical. Ashamed for him,
DAWN BIRDCATCHER *moves closer to* MR
TABUTANZER.

This innocence is the stumbling block.

MR TABUTANZER. There must be an outcome. The complaint
has to be processed one way or another. If your report had
not been inconclusive…

TRUMAN. It wasn't inconclusive. There wasn't sufficient
evidence.

MR TABUTANZER. And here's our problem. This business
can't be resolved in the old way. You're right, to dispose of
her like this is worse than meaningless. This innocence can
only travel.

They look out towards the smoke.

And there are plenty more like her, out there. Young.

DAWN BIRDCATCHER. It's hopeless.

TRUMAN. The world's changing so fast. I don't understand it.

DAWN BIRDCATCHER. Nor do I. And I take *Newsweek*.

TRUMAN. It's driven me mad! There's nothing about her that's tangibly objectionable. No ideology. No book or manifesto at her heart. I've woken at nights dreaming she was a jihadist, her breasts explosives... a fantasy. There is nothing there to apprehend.

MR TABUTANZER. And yet there is a way.

MR TABUTANZER continues to wait for his moment, enjoying himself.

Are you devoted to the Society?

TRUMAN. I swore my allegiance.

MR TABUTANZER. Take this and tie one of his hands to the chair.

He hands DAWN BIRDCATCHER *a noose on a length of rope.*

DAWN BIRDCATCHER. Hmm?

MR TABUTANZER. All will be clear.

As she does so, the noose tightening around TRUMAN*'s wrist...*

Our problem is that the complaint has penetrated the Society. More serious, the complainer and complaint have become fused. The Society cannot eject the complaint without also ejecting the person, and to do so, one way or another, is to create more grounds for complaint. Now she's listening.

AFRA *immediately covers for this.* TRUMAN *has now been attached to the chair by the cord.*

When a body is invaded, what must it do? What does any body do? It sends a cell to attach itself to the invader and thereby alter its pernicious character. This is the sacrifice that will resolve the problem. Following the laws laid down by the ancients, who knew that only sacrifice can ensure the moral balance of a Society.

He tilts AFRA*'s chair over the edge.* TRUMAN *scrabbles frantically at the cord at his wrist.*

That knot will not loosen. What will they find below? Once they have separated the explosion of blood and bone, sinew and fat? The two sides of this conflict locked together in a tragedy that neither could escape. And therefore neither will be the point of blame.

TRUMAN. The theory is good.

MR TABUTANZER. What is conflict after all? What are wars? But a sacrifice – that, by a letting of blood by both sides, cleanses the victor of guilt.

From here MR TABUTANZER *steps back, the ringmaster, observing indulgently.*

DAWN BIRDCATCHER. No!

TRUMAN. Don't stop me!

DAWN BIRDCATCHER. You mustn't!

TRUMAN. I am ready!

DAWN BIRDCATCHER. You haven't considered the emotional consequences.

TRUMAN. I shall be dead. A martyr to the Society...

DAWN BIRDCATCHER. What about me? What will this do to me? Have you thought of that? How can I continue my affair with Mr Tabutanzer carrying the burden of your martyrdom? Have you thought of anyone but yourselves? How can I look Mr Tabutanzer's children in the eye knowing their mother is harbouring the guilt of a sacrificed husband? You men rush headlong in with your ideas but never think of the human consequences. Has there been a proper consultation process? Have all affected parties been canvassed? You don't even know the opinions of your target demographic, even at the anecdotal level. Have you even asked her for her perspective? No. She's gagged, which, I think, says it all.

TRUMAN *steps back from the edge.*

MR TABUTANZER. Of course, Miss Birdcatcher's right. We have not observed process. We ought to hear all sides.

He indicates the gag to be taken off.

DAWN BIRDCATCHER (*removing the gag*). Tell them what you think.

AFRA *looks at all of them, with a calm, steely eye.*

AFRA. I only want to see through my complaint.

After a moment.

MR TABUTANZER. And you shall. I shall confess something. I've played a game with you, to lead you to where we can... (*Conjuring.*) next-level.

TRUMAN. Next-level?

MR TABUTANZER. I bring many new words from the gathering in the desert. Powerful words. That is only one of them. Two of them. Hyphenated. I knew you wouldn't sacrifice yourself. How? Because you haven't done the paperwork. It's not in your nature. It's not in any of our natures. We are Administrators.

MR TABUTANZER *takes off his robes to reveal an extremely sharp suit beneath them, of a deep 'administration blue'. He should appear to almost shine in it, like a saint.*

I ordered two suits. Tweed for casual, this for day. They say a man is known by his clothes. Together, in that desert, amongst the gathering of our kind, drawn from the corners of the earth, none there looking out across that sea of administrators, could deny we were... A PEOPLE.

DAWN BIRDCATCHER *and* TRUMAN *seem transfixed by his tone and presence.*

DAWN BIRDCATCHER. You look wonderful...

MR TABUTANZER. Now you are ready to hear the message I bring from the desert. How we, together, may take this terrible problem our Society is facing... and *transform* it.

DAWN BIRDCATCHER. With magic!?

MR TABUTANZER. A sort of magic. But I am not a revolutionary. I am a *so*lutionary. That's another word you can use.

He producing a pocket knife and cuts the cord tying TRUMAN *to the chair.*

(*To* TRUMAN.) Go to my office. Bring the portrait of President King.

TRUMAN *goes.*

When he is gone MR TABUTANZER *and* DAWN BIRDCATCHER *embrace.*

DAWN BIRDCATCHER. It's intoxicating.

MR TABUTANZER. Revolutions are intoxicating.

DAWN BIRDCATCHER. *So*lutions.

MR TABUTANZER. Solutions. Are intoxicating.

They kiss.

There, did you feel that? The summer wind.

They start mopping their brows.

DAWN BIRDCATCHER. It's like it's alive.

Music over, coming as if from the street below, at the back of the building, as MR TABUTANZER *and* DAWN BIRDCATCHER *remove their outer clothing.*

Scene Twelve

The same, night. The stars are fully out across the sky, and we can hear the sound of cicadas. All are sitting, now in minimal clothing in the sudden heat. AFRA is still tied to her chair, and TRUMAN holds the framed portrait of President King. Both he and DAWN BIRDCATCHER are enrapt as MR TABUTANZER, glowing in the moonlight, holds forth, now and then referring to scribbled notes on scraps of paper in his hand.

MR TABUTANZER. And then the Speaker spoke about states and nations. He said… there is a crisis of administration among the nations of the world. Why? Because their time is past. Their reason-to-be was to protect their people from greater nations than themselves, and so they grew, and grew. But today these nations have no devil at their gate. And so they shall become One Nation, and the administrators of those nations shall become One People arching over them, and together we will find a new devil… if we look for it long enough… (*Gazing up at the stars.*)

So spake the Speaker shining in the moonlight, his white hair flowing. He came in a white suit and spoke for three hours without notes, in his shirtsleeves. He wore sandals, and he was called Cleve or Steve… or something like that, with a 'v' in it… but his name is not important. It is not important.

And he continued, as we sat as you are sitting now, like children, astonished by his truth. 'The Nations are being replaced by the chaos of humanity, now linked one-to-another by personal communicators. This seething, unthinking mass of humanity would take the world back a thousand years, to the land, to clans, and tribes… (*Checking his notes.*) to a New Age of Ignorance. All that stands between this and disaster… is… *us*. Order's Redeemers. The Administrators of the World! THOSE WHO GET OTHERS TO WORK!

DAWN BIRDCATCHER. Yes! Yes!

MR TABUTANZER. A great cheer went up from the gathering. Some wept openly. He went on... 'So we come together, here in the desert, from the four corners of the Earth, to share and acknowledge this Great Work.'

TRUMAN. What is the work?

MR TABUTANZER. You ask the question. Then you are ready to hear the answer. Just as we were ready. And so together, we recited the Administrator's Prayer... Where there's strife we shall inherit... Yes, yes, repeat it after me... Where there is danger and fear...

MR TABUTANZER / TRUMAN / DAWN BIRDCATCHER (*uncertainly*)....we shall inherit.

MR TABUTANZER. Where the world is unmanageable...

MR TABUTANZER / TRUMAN / DAWN BIRDCATCHER. ...we shall inherit.

MR TABUTANZER. Where the earth is toxic...

TRUMAN / DAWN BIRDCATCHER....we shall inherit.

MR TABUTANZER. I've paraphrased... (*Consulting his notes.*) I have not done his words justice... he said it so much better than I.

DAWN BIRDCATCHER. We understand. What must we do now?

MR TABUTANZER. Bring me the portrait of President King.

TRUMAN, *who had forgotten he was holding it, presents it, but* MR TABUTANZER *does not take it.*

Throw it over the edge.

Both TRUMAN *and* DAWN BIRDCATCHER *are speechless.*

Throw it over! Let it fall to the ground and shatter, where it will be seen by all who enter or leave this building. Where they will tread on its broken pieces. Throw it down.

DAWN BIRDCATCHER. What are you saying?

MR TABUTANZER. Administrators of the World! (*From his notes*.) Sometimes the Earth's plates snap to a new configuration, bringing disaster and opportunity. We must not run from the great wave that imperils us, but swim towards it and meet it out beyond the shallows before it rears to its deadly height! If we can do that, this is our moment to inherit the world. But to do it we must not look up, but DOWN! UPON THE PEOPLE! AS ONE!

DAWN BIRDCATCHER *takes the portrait, goes to the front of the building (upstage) and throws it over the edge. After a couple of seconds we hear a smash of its glass on the ground below.*

DAWN BIRDCATCHER. I did it! (*Elated, excited, a little alarmed*.)

MR TABUTANZER. It's done.

TRUMAN. What has she done?

MR TABUTANZER *takes his time, laughing, relaxed.*

MR TABUTANZER. What do you make of this?

AFRA. I don't believe it's real. This change is too quick, like a dream.

MR TABUTANZER. She's befaddled. Who can blame her? How much has this brave woman suffered, still patiently sitting in her chair? The fortitude, the persistence, and forbearance in her heroic suppression of her self?

After each question, he waits and searches AFRA*'s face for a reaction.*

What emotions have been passing through her mind? What thoughts has she been hiding? To have repressed so much? We must protect her with our lives!

TRUMAN (*still stunned, peering down*). We'll all be strung up.

MR TABUTANZER. The Speaker talked about fear. Of changes in societies like ours and how we must face them. But we are in position. (*At* DAWN BIRDCATCHER.) Isn't what you've done, in your own way, by throwing the President from the roof, is that not also a sort of complaint?

DAWN BIRDCATCHER. Yes!

MR TABUTANZER. And if any make objection to it, won't they also be complaining too? Then we, the Administrators, shall handle it in our way. And thus, in this momentous time of change and uncertainty WE SHALL PREVAIL. Fetch me a DV8... and-a-half.

DAWN BIRDCATCHER (*stopping, having already half gone*). And-a-half?

He nods, meaningfully. She goes again, excited.

MR TABUTANZER. Untie her.

TRUMAN *does so.*

What's the matter?

TRUMAN. To rule without fear...!

MR TABUTANZER. There's no going back.

TRUMAN. Fear is government.

MR TABUTANZER. Was. No longer.

TRUMAN. I had her and you stopped me.

MR TABUTANZER. Go and draft a complaint on our headed paper, the nice stuff, so it's known that our department was the first to complain about the mess below, and the danger it poses to public health. We cannot have glass spread across the pavement!

TRUMAN. No. No we can't.

Smiles, seeing MR TABUTANZER's *brilliance.*

MR TABUTANZER. Now get out of my sight.

TRUMAN. Yes.

TRUMAN *starts to go, a shuffling, bewildered little man, holding on to a hope. He passes* DAWN BIRDCATCHER, *who is very out of breath, returning with a stapled form in an envelope. She and* TRUMAN *exchange looks that also include* MR TABUTANZER. TRUMAN *exits.*

MR TABUTANZER. Miss Birdcatcher.

DAWN BIRDCATCHER. Mr Tabutanzer.

MR TABUTANZER. You wish to say something to me.

DAWN BIRDCATCHER. I just wanted to thank you, Mr Tabutanzer.

MR TABUTANZER. No no no…

DAWN BIRDCATCHER.…for giving me this opportunity.

MR TABUTANZER. I've done nothing.

DAWN BIRDCATCHER. This is the first time in my life that I've incriminated myself for someone else's benefit entirely of my own free will.

They kiss.

MR TABUTANZER. I shall leave you to untie her, and neatly tie up everything else without exception. (*To* AFRA.) You are free. (*With a bow.*) It has been a great pleasure to represent you.

MR TABUTANZER *exits.* DAWN BIRDCATCHER *comes forward, produces a pen and the form, filling out the name on the top.*

DAWN BIRDCATCHER. Were you generally satisfied with the outcome of your complaint?

AFRA (*after a moment*). Yes.

DAWN BIRDCATCHER (*fills it in, as after*). Was there anything in the way your complaint was dealt with that you felt could have been improved?

AFRA. No.

DAWN BIRDCATCHER. Was the process generally clear and understandable?

AFRA. Yes.

DAWN BIRDCATCHER. Were those who dealt with your complaint polite and helpful?

AFRA. Yes. At times.

DAWN BIRDCATCHER. Have you suffered any permanent injury or damage during the process of your complaint?

AFRA. No.

DAWN BIRDCATCHER. Have you suffered death or loss of property as a result of the processing of your complaint?

AFRA. No.

DAWN BIRDCATCHER. Would you recommend bringing a complaint to the Society to anyone you know? If the answer to this question is 'no' please state briefly why.

AFRA. I'd rather not say.

DAWN BIRDCATCHER. If you would rather not say please explain briefly why.

AFRA. No.

After a moment of reading on...

DAWN BIRDCATCHER. If your answer to this question is also 'no' please go to the last section... (*Turns pages.*) You may, but are not required to, use the space provided to explain why you are applying to be part of the administration.

AFRA. But I'm not applying to the administration.

DAWN BIRDCATCHER. No. No, you appear not to be, I agree. I suppose you should leave it blank in that case, shouldn't you? Leave that space blank.

AFRA *looks at* DAWN BIRDCATCHER *and at the form, then takes the pen offered to her, removed from its sterilised wrapper.*

Don't touch the paper!

AFRA *doesn't, and signs.* DAWN BIRDCATCHER *takes the form, and exits.*

After a moment, AFRA *checks to see she is alone. When she's sure, a change seems to come over her. She looks out in the direction of where the smoke was coming from.*

We hear a very distant, deep explosion.

Music (the same as early in the play) starts drifting up from a nearby building.

AFRA *reaches into her shoe, takes out half a cigarette, and lights it. She smokes, listening to the music. As she does so, her face should appear to change, and we should feel, for the first time, that we might read her thoughts. These thoughts are full of conflicts: relief, determination, weariness but above all, and predominantly, doubt.*

She finishes the cigarette after a few puffs, puts it out, and sits for a moment more, reflecting. She takes a deep breath to calm herself but starts to cry instead, before quickly controlling herself again. She dries and cleans her eyes, and takes a tiny mirror from her other shoe to check her eyes are clear.

She stands, visibly re-gathers herself, and turns back into the character we have known, before exiting from the roof.

The music finishes. Another very distant, almost subliminally deep, explosion can just be heard in the far distance, followed by a silence.

Blackout.